GREAT UNSOLVED MYSTERIES

On Treasure's Trail
by Jessica Schulte

MYSTERIES OF HISTORY
by Katherine Scraper

GLOBE FEARON

Pearson Learning Group

Contents

On Treasure's Trail

MYSTERIES OF HISTORY

On Treasure's Trail

by Jessica Schulte

Chapter 1

The Lure of Treasure

Imagine you are walking along on a sidewalk near your home. You see a sheet of paper at your feet. Your curiosity makes you pick up the paper. In your hands is a yellowed map with a big black **X** on it. Could the **X** mark the spot of a pirate's treasure chest? Is there a fortune to be found? Your imagination kicks into gear.

Picture yourself on television, talking about your success. You get **credit** for discovering a huge fortune. What a wonderful daydream. It's easy to see why people dream of finding treasure.

Treasure doesn't always come in pirates' chests. There aren't always maps to follow. Sometimes treasure hunters look for clues to help solve a mystery. Good treasure hunters must know the story behind a treasure. Details of the past may reveal important clues to help track down a treasure. Following clues, understanding history, and having a dream to find something special keep treasure hunters going day after day.

Seeking Treasure

You have probably heard tales of chests overflowing with jewels and gold pieces. However, treasure doesn't have to be worth a lot of money. A cuddly teddy bear might be a treasure to a child. An old family photo could be one to an elderly person. An ancient statue, missing arms and worn with age, can be a valuable treasure, too. It is a piece of history. Scientists can study the statue to understand how people lived thousands of years ago. People **refer** to the statue as valuable because it can't be replaced.

Treasure hunters must learn all they can if they want to increase their chances of finding treasure. One place to begin is to look into the past. For instance, old diaries, letters, and maps might offer clues. In some cases, treasure hunters have to figure out secret codes.

It's important to believe in the search. A strong belief helps a treasure hunter keep going. Sometimes, though, people look for treasures that might not have really existed. For example, legends about pirate treasure or lost gold mines are told over and over. Nobody is really sure if the stories are true. However, because the treasures in certain stories have not been found, people **extend** their searches. They hope that one of the legends or stories will offer a clue that leads to a special treasure.

This elaborate gold statue represents amazing ceremonies that may—or may not—have taken place long ago.

Long ago, explorers traveled to new lands and returned home with amazing stories of entire cities made of gold and lakes filled with jewels. Were these stories true? Nobody knows for sure. Even when the stories haven't proved to be true, people still want to believe that the treasures exist. They spend years searching, following clues.

However, some treasure is real. After its discovery, it is appreciated by many people, perhaps in a museum. In this book, you will read about two kinds of stories about treasure—legends and true tales. You will also read about how the search for treasure can lead to danger, or even death.

The Glow of El Dorado

What would you think if you heard about a man covered from head to toe with glittering gold dust? Spanish explorers returned from South America in the mid 1500s describing such a man. The explorers described a king they called El Dorado, which means "the golden one" in Spanish. The explorers said the land they explored was filled with gold. They called the land El Dorado as well. There was no proof of any riches. Yet people wanted to believe the stories were true. Soon after hearing about the gold king, the king of Spain sent conquistadors to South America. These men were to claim the gold-filled lands for Spain as a **conquest** and rule the people who lived there.

The conquistadors returned to tell amazing stories. For example, the men described a king who was covered in gold dust. The king would row into the middle of a lake. He'd wash the gold dust from his body. Then, the king would throw jewelry and precious stones into the lake. The jewels would sink out of sight to the bottom.

The conquistadors wondered how much gold was in the lake. They planned to go to the lake to drain it and take the gold back to Spain. The conquistadors wanted to take **credit** for finding the gold and become rich, too.

The number of stories began to **increase**. Some tales told of a shimmering golden city nestled deep in the jungle. Can you imagine a city made of gold? It was said that the gold walls reflected the sun so brightly that people had to squint their eyes to keep the sight from hurting them.

Seekers of El Dorado

Spanish treasure hunters were eager to reach South America. They wanted to claim the golden city for their king. One treasure-hunting trip was to the area in South America that is known today as Ecuador. In the 1570s, a Spanish explorer named Pérez de Quesada looked for a native people called the Waipis. Quesada believed that they would know where the city of El Dorado was.

Quesada did meet the Waipis, but they didn't help the Spaniards. In fact, the Waipis attacked and killed five of Quesada's men. Quesada did not let the Waipis **defeat** his spirit. He believed that he was getting closer to his goal. Quesada thought the Waipis attacked because they wanted to protect and **preserve** El Dorado. Quesada kept looking for the city of gold, but he never found it.

Spaniards weren't the only people who wanted to find the treasure of El Dorado. English people wanted to find gold, too. In 1595, the English explorer and soldier Sir Walter Raleigh heard of great riches in the Americas. He learned that a fortune was hidden in the newly explored land on the other side of the Atlantic Ocean. Raleigh did not want Spain to find the treasure first. He asked his queen to let him go to Guiana in South America. That is where Raleigh thought the golden city was located. The queen of England agreed to the trip.

Sir Walter Raleigh treated the native peoples he met with courtesy. He **extended** peace to them and won their trust. However, he did not find the city of gold. Out of supplies, Raleigh returned to England to ask the queen to pay for more supplies for another attempt to make a **conquest**. He wanted to go back to South America to keep looking for El Dorado. The queen refused to give Raleigh the money he needed.

Not all of the trips made in order to locate the city of El Dorado took place in the sixteenth century. For instance, in 1925, English colonel Percy Fawcett, his son Jack, and a friend named Raleigh Rimme decided to try to find the place by themselves. These treasure hunters searched for El Dorado in Brazil. They used a **historic** map that had been created in the 1700s. This map showed the way to a lost city. The men thought this city might be El Dorado. It is known that the three entered the Brazilian jungle, but they were never seen or heard from again.

There was talk that Fawcett's team really did find El Dorado. According to this story, the three men were being held prisoner there. Their captivity would keep them from spreading the word about the lost city. Nobody would be able to **plunder**, or rob and destroy, the city. Rescue teams were sent to find the three men. The teams never found them. To this day, nobody knows what happened to the men.

Some people think that the lost city may be located in Peru, a country in South America. There have been recent findings that **refer** to the Incas, a people who lived in Peru a long time ago. The Incas were known for making fine gold jewelry and decorations. They had well-planned cities with roads and waterways between them. A number of Inca buildings have lasted more than 500 years. Some historians think that when the Spaniards invaded Peru, the Incas fled to a secret city. They went there to avoid a **conquest**.

The Spaniards never found the Incas. An explorer named Hiram Bingham later discovered what was left of the secret city, called Machu Picchu, in 1911. Nothing had ever been written about it.

Machu Picchu is now open to visitors. Many people visit Peru each year to see this **historic** Incan city. Could it be a clue to the mystery of El Dorado? Maybe there are other ancient cities that are still **preserved**. Perhaps El Dorado was actually another Incan city, hidden deep within the mountains of Peru, still waiting to be found.

Many people share the dream of discovering the treasures of El Dorado. Some explorers get lost in the jungle. Some get sick from snakebites. In fact, some people even die while looking for the city. No one has found anything that proves El Dorado is in Peru. El Dorado was first spoken of hundreds of years ago. Yet its mystery still tempts many treasure seekers today.

Are these ancient ruins the secret city of gold?

Chapter 3

The Money Pit

It was 1795, and 16-year-old Daniel McGinnis had a plan. He had decided to explore Oak Island. The island is just off the coast of Nova Scotia in Canada. Nobody had lived on the island for as long as McGinnis—or anyone in his town—could remember. Even so, for years and years before McGinnis was born, people had talked of seeing flickering lights on Oak Island. McGinnis was curious. There was a legend that the famous pirate Captain Kidd had buried his treasure somewhere nearby. Could Captain Kidd's treasure be buried on Oak Island? Maybe the pirate haunted the island. Perhaps the flickering lights would lead McGinnis to the pirate's buried treasure! There were many ideas **revolving** in McGinnis's mind.

McGinnis paddled to the island to explore. He walked through a wooded area. He came upon a clearing. McGinnis noticed something right away. There were tree stumps in the clearing. He thought to himself, "If nobody lived on the island, then who had cut the trees?" McGinnis looked more closely. He noticed a large circular dent in the ground. It looked as if a giant hole had been dug and then filled in. McGinnis wondered whether a well had been dug there. However, as nobody lived on the island, McGinnis didn't think that was the answer. There would be no need for a well to provide water if nobody lived on the island.

McGinnis had an idea. He thought that the circle might have been where Captain Kidd left his treasure. In 1701, Kidd was hanged for crimes on the seas. Before his trial, Kidd was said to have buried a chest full of treasure. McGinnis knew he had to uncover it.

Digging for Treasure

Excited, McGinnis went back home and **informed** two friends about what he had found on the island. Anthony Vaughan and John Smith were just as eager as McGinnis to begin digging up the treasure. The next day, they arrived on the island with shovels and picks. They reached the clearing and began to dig.

They dug about 2 feet down and hit something hard. It turned out to be a layer of flat stones, called flagstones. It seemed as if someone had thought to **insert** the stones there on purpose. The boys thought the stones were supposed to discourage anybody who might come across the site and try to dig for treasure. They saw this as proof that something very special must be at the bottom of the hole.

McGinnis and his friends called their new discovery "the Money Pit." The boys were sure they would **profit** when they uncovered whatever had been hidden in the hole. They were eager to find treasure.

The boys continued digging. They reached 10 feet into the hole and hit another barrier. This time it was a platform made of oak. They were able to remove it and continue their dig. They hit another layer of oak at 20 feet and again at 30. Someone had gone to a lot of trouble to make sure that whatever was buried in the hole would remain safe.

The three boys knew they couldn't dig any farther on their own. McGinnis and his two friends realized they needed help. They were too poor to hire people to help them. So the boys made a plan. They knew that they needed to convince others that there was treasure on Oak Island. They decided they would raise enough money to return to the island and finally solve the mystery.

THE MONEY PIT
in 1803

flagstones at 2 feet

10 ft. —

oak platforms

20 ft. —

30 ft. —

40 ft. —

50 ft. —

coconut fibers at 55 feet

60 ft. —

oak platforms

70 ft. —

80 ft. —

stone with message carved on it at 90 feet

90 ft. —

wood at 98 feet

metal below 98 feet

12

It took 8 years for McGinnis and his friends to return to the Money Pit with more workers and tools. They dug deeper than before and discovered that there were even more oak platforms in their way. Then, at about 55 feet, they hit a layer of coconut fiber. Where did it come from? There were no coconut trees close to Nova Scotia. Perhaps the coconut fiber had come from far away, from a country that a pirate had visited. The searchers thought that the fiber was a clue. They thought it was more proof that a treasure chest laid buried in the pit.

McGinnis's team also found a stone with a strange code carved into it. As the treasure hunters kept going, they noticed the soil was becoming muddy. Then, when they were about 98 feet into the hole, they hit something hard. They thought they must be close to the treasure so they stopped for the night. When the group came back in the morning, the hole had filled with water. Now, there was no way the treasure hunters could finish their search.

Deeper Into the Pit

By 1849, Daniel McGinnis was dead. However, his friends were still determined to get to the bottom of the Money Pit mystery. The men did not allow the puzzle to **defeat** them. They returned with different helpers and more tools to help reach the treasure.

This new team brought something extra. They had a drill with a hollow bit. The new tool could bring up little pieces of whatever material it went through. The treasure hunters would be able to tell what was beneath the water by studying the material the drill brought up to them.

The drill was **inserted** into the pit. It went down past the water. Beneath the water, there were many layers of different kinds of wood. The team also discovered 22 inches of metal. Beneath the metal, there were even more layers of wood. The treasure hunters thought this meant that there were *two* treasure chests to **recover**.

The team learned something else about the Money Pit. It appeared that when it was first built, someone made it so the pit would flood on purpose. The explorers discovered a system of tunnels on the nearby beach. These tunnels sucked in the water from the ocean and then led the water underground into the pit. This meant the level of the water in the Money Pit would **increase** at different times throughout the day and would never go away. No one would ever be able to dig all the way down to get to whatever was at the bottom of the pit. It was impossible to dig without hitting water. The treasure hunters tried everything they could to stop the tunnels from taking water to the hole. It was no use. No matter what they tried, nothing worked.

Was there any way to continue the search for treasure?

The Challenge Continues

It was soon discovered that there were two different tunnels that led to the Money Pit. One was from Smith's Cove. The other tunnel came from the South Shore Cove. This design meant that no one could ever **extend** the dig past a certain point. Sea water would flood the pit, making it impossible to explore.

Many different teams and treasure hunters have gone to Oak Island to try to get to the treasure. Everyone has tried a different method to reach whatever is at the bottom of this deep hole. New shafts were dug next to the first pit in order to avoid flooding. That didn't work. No matter how the diggers tried to stop the water from filling the hole, it filled again and again.

Many machines dug fast and deep into the earth but came up with nothing. Skin divers were brought in to swim to the bottom but were unable to find anything. Dynamite was used to try to blast the pit wide open. In 1965, a modern causeway was built to connect the island to the mainland in order to allow people to get to Oak Island quickly. Several men died trying to get to the hoped-for treasure. So far, every attempt to reach it has failed.

Treasure hunters have been trying different ways to get to the bottom of the Money Pit for hundreds of years. They spend time and effort asking other people to give them money to help them. They dig as long as their money lasts. Then, they go back home and try to prove that they are getting closer to a discovery. Next, the treasure hunters raise more money so that they can go back to Oak Island.

People are still trying to get to the bottom of the hole. The Money Pit was first discovered more than 200 years ago. Even today, it remains a mystery.

A Clue?

Do you remember the stone with carving on it that was found in the Money Pit? The secret message was decoded. Many people believed that the stone said, "Forty feet below, 2 million pounds are buried." Pounds are English money, so 2 million pounds means a lot of money. This news made some people very excited. They were sure that the message on the stone was proof that there was treasure at the bottom of the hole. They wanted to keep digging.

Others thought the explorers were making up this message. The treasure hunters had run out of money. They wanted to raise more money to begin another attempt to reach the treasure in the Money Pit. Was this a trick? Would the treasure hunters lie to **profit** by the search? Maybe the idea was that people would donate money to the treasure hunters if they had more proof that the treasure was real.

However, the stone was lost after its message was reported so its message cannot be checked. Some people wonder if the stone's message really **referred** to buried treasure. If not, what else could it mean? The missing stone is one more mystery in the story of the Money Pit.

Do you think there is a treasure waiting to be found in the Money Pit?

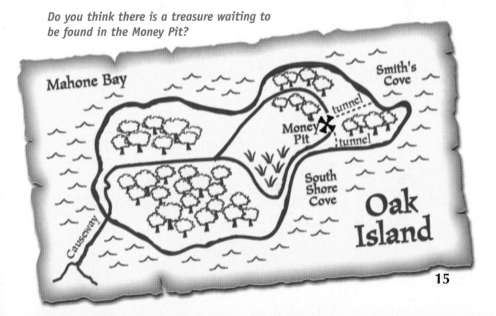

Chapter 4

Missing Confederate Gold

The next story is about a famous treasure that disappeared. In April 1865, the American Civil War was coming to an end after four long years. The war was between the North and the South. The South wanted to become its own country. Jefferson Davis was the president of the South, which was also called the Confederacy. Davis was worried that the North was going to **defeat** the South. Homes had been **plundered**. Farms were destroyed. Roads and bridges were wiped out. Only one railroad line worked. The war had brought ruin to the South.

However, President Davis had an important treasure. He had a lot of money he had borrowed from a bank in France to pay for the war. Davis met with his top men to **inform** them of his plans for returning the money. He had promised to repay the loan even if the Confederacy lost the war. After the loan was repaid, there would still be some money left over. It could be used to help the South **recover** from the war.

Davis told his men that he, his wife, and his cabinet members would take one train from Richmond, Virginia, to Danville, Virginia, on the border of North Carolina. Another train was for William H. Parker, a captain of the Confederate navy. Parker's train would carry a **quantity** of boxes of gold pieces, silver coins, solid gold bricks, and cash to the U.S. Mint in Charlotte, North Carolina, where it could be safely stored.

Captain Parker knew that he would have to work hard to guard the treasure. He would have to stay alert and keep moving to stay ahead of people who might be after the treasure. There were many desperate Southerners who might try to rob the train. Northern soldiers might attack as well.

Many railroad lines were destroyed during the Civil War.

Parker needed help. He asked sailors who were on a boat outside of Richmond to help him guard the treasure. Some of these sailors were just young boys.

Traveling by train was not a simple matter. Many Southern railroad tracks had been destroyed by the Northern **military**. The train could only take its riders part of the distance to Anderson, South Carolina. Parker's men were forced to march by foot for the remainder of the trip. They carried the treasure with them in wagons. Parker headed for North Carolina to the U.S. Mint in Charlotte to deliver the money to safety.

When Parker arrived at the mint, he was **informed** that the Northern army was heading to North Carolina. That news meant that the Confederate gold would not be safe if it was left in the mint. The troops had to keep moving. They disguised the wagons carrying the treasure. They built a false bottom in the wagons' floor. Underneath what looked like a plain wooden floor was another floor. That's where the treasure was hidden. If the Northern **military** stopped Parker's force, Northern soldiers would be fooled into thinking there was nothing valuable in the wagons.

The Lost Gold

Parker made his way to Washington, Georgia. Some historians believe that Parker arrived at the Chennault Plantation there. It is said he camped at the edge of the plantation, which was a large farm owned by the Chennault family. Parker received new orders while camped. He was **informed** that he had to go to Savannah to see President Davis. There they would have a meeting and Parker would be told what to do next.

On his way to meet Davis, Parker learned that the Northern troops were nearby. Parker had no choice. He had to turn around and go back to the plantation.

A popular version of the story that many people believe is that just 100 yards away from the front porch of the plantation house, Parker's group was attacked. The wagons were robbed. The attackers snatched the gold and other valuables that they found. They rode off with bags stuffed with treasure tied to their saddles. There was so much treasure that it was said to drop to the ground as the robbers galloped away across the county.

Some people thought that the horses couldn't carry such heavy loads for long. Others thought the robbers had to have stopped to bury the treasure in the nearby swamps and forests. However, the Confederate gold was never seen again.

On May 10, 1865, President Jefferson Davis was captured by the Northern troops. He did not have the treasure with him. The bank in France never received its payment. What happened to the treasure hidden in the false bottoms of the wagons? Even with such careful plans to keep it safe and move it through the South, it seemed as if the treasure had disappeared.

The Northern troops believed that the treasure was hidden somewhere on the plantation. The soldiers searched the grounds. No gold was found. The soldiers looked through the house. They didn't find any gold there, either. Even though there was no trace of gold or money, the Northern soldiers were sure that the Southern troops had buried the treasure on the plantation. The soldiers **increased** their questioning of the Chennault family, but no one knew about the lost treasure. The family was sent to Washington, D.C., for questioning. When no new clues were found, the Chennaults were finally allowed to return to their home.

Tales of riches at the "golden farm" began to spread around the country. Soon, people traveled long distances to visit the plantation. They wanted to try to find the buried treasure on the plantation's property. It was said that when there was a heavy rain, gold coins were easy to find along the paths and roads of the place.

Wagons like this one held Confederate gold.

The Captain's Version

The tales about what happened to the South's gold upset Captain Parker. He said that nobody was telling the truth. Parker wanted to **inform** people about what happened. He wanted to set the record straight. The captain wanted **credit** for protecting the South's treasure. He wanted the world to know that the gold was not stolen while he was in charge. Parker wrote to a newspaper in 1893 with his version of the events. He told a very different story.

Parker wrote that he believed President Davis took some **quantity** of the gold. Parker thought Davis wanted to use it for the South's government and the **recovery** from the war. However, the main portion of the fortune remained with Captain Parker.

Parker said he took the gold to the old mint in North Carolina, thinking it would be safe there. Then, learning that the Northern army was near, he decided to move the money to Georgia. The treasure was moved in a "train" of wagons. The soldiers and Parker himself followed the wagons on foot. They kept moving as quickly as they could.

For some reason, as Parker and his men made their journey, at each place they arrived, people were waiting to see them. It was as if people expected them. Parker was puzzled. How did the word get out? None of his men ever went ahead of the wagons. Yet somehow people seemed to know that Parker's men were traveling with gold. Even though so many people knew about the treasure, Captain Parker claimed he kept it safe.

Parker wrote that he heard that the Northern army was getting closer. He knew he had to **increase** his speed to stay ahead of the enemy. He ordered his troops to "lighten the load" so they could move faster. The men began to toss things off the wagons.

Were Parker's troops so frightened that they did not pay attention to what they threw away? In their hurry, perhaps the soldiers threw out the Confederate gold. Yet, is that likely if the treasure was hidden in the wagons' false bottoms?

Parker's account of what happened does not agree with the popular story told in the time following the Civil War. Captain Parker said that he went to Washington, Georgia. Yet he never said that he went to a plantation. He did not **refer** to being robbed or attacked. Parker insisted that the money remained in the wagons. When he had to put the gold in a warehouse to keep it safe, a soldier stood guard. Townsmen threatened to break in. However, the guard did his job. He did not let anything happen to the money. The treasure remained in Georgia for three days. Then, while in Augusta, Georgia, Parker was **informed** that Northern troops were coming. He moved the money back to the wagons. He was ready to travel somewhere else in order to keep the treasure safe.

Parker said he received new orders before he left. He was told to deliver the treasure to General Duke in Abbeville, South Carolina. Parker claimed that he turned over the money to the general in Abbeville, that the treasure was safely delivered. He said that for 30 days, Confederate soldiers and sailors had guarded and protected the treasure.

Who Lost the Gold?

According to one version of the story, the gold was stolen at the plantation. Captain Parker's story is different. He claimed that he never lost sight of the treasure in his care. He insisted that he took good care of the treasure. The two stories do not match.

Treasure hunters must be able to listen to different stories of the same event. Then, they must figure out what they believe. If you were hunting for the lost Confederate treasure, whom would you believe? Was there a reason for Captain Parker to lie? Why did he wait 28 years to tell his story? What about the Chennaults? Could they have known where the gold was buried? Perhaps the thieves were local people. Could they have divided the gold and given it away to their friends and family? The Civil War had left many people desperate. There were no jobs, and many families' homes had been destroyed. That money was needed by a lot of people. Think about this: If Parker's men had been robbed, wouldn't some of the treasure have shown up when the money was spent?

There are other possibilities, too. Perhaps the money was left in the swamps where the Apalachee and Oconee rivers meet. Maybe whoever hid it there went back later to **recover** it. Could the bags of loot have been left behind somewhere? Could something else have been packed in all those crates and boxes that Parker was guarding? Was the treasure even real?

The mystery is still unsolved. Civil War scholars, scientists, and treasure hunters still comb through the story looking for clues and facts. Visitors can stay at the **historic** Chennault Plantation in Georgia and try their luck at finding the lost treasure.

What do you think happened to the Confederate gold?

Chapter 5

A Lost Gold Mine

Like the other tales you have read, the next story tells about a missing treasure. This treasure was pure gold. However, there is more to this mystery than disappearing gold. Not only is the gold itself missing, but also the original location of the treasure has never been found. According to legend, the gold was first discovered in a mine in the Superstition Mountains, east of present-day Phoenix, Arizona. This mine is known as the Lost Dutchman Mine. There are many different versions of what happened to the mine and the gold it held. The puzzling details of the story change with each new telling. It is a mystery that began long ago but still tempts treasure seekers into the mountains in search of gold.

One version of the legend tells of the Peraltas, a Mexican family that found the mine first. It was some time in the 1840s. The Peraltas had found some places to mine. They were able to make a living with the gold they found.

On their last mining trip, they found the richest gold mine ever. The Peraltas took as much gold as they could carry. It seemed as if the Peraltas would get rich from this treasure. Before they were able to return home, tragedy struck. Some Apaches, Native Americans who lived in the area, attacked the group. The Apaches did not want the Peraltas to take away the gold. Two members of the Peralta family survived the attack.

When the survivors made it back home, they told others about the mine. They said there was a mountain shaped like a hat by the mine. Although it was easy to locate the mountain, nobody ever found the mine.

Weiser and Waltz and the Mine

Many years after the Peraltas had been attacked, two men from Germany made their way to what is now Arizona. Jacob Weiser and Jacob Waltz had come to America to get rich. The men planned that their new life would **revolve** around digging for gold.

Some stories say that Weiser and Waltz met one of the Peraltas who lived through the attack. This man told the two Germans about the gold in the mountains. Some stories say that the two immigrants found the mine on their own. No matter how the men got to it, they found a mine that was filled with gold.

The two men went to work right away. They stored their gold in a hiding place close to the mine. That way they would never have to carry large amounts of gold at any one time. The idea was that if they hid the gold and only handled small amounts at a time, the main treasure would be protected from robbers. If either of them were robbed, the thieves would never get away with a lot of gold.

After the two partners started to work the mine, Weiser was mysteriously killed. It isn't clear how it happened. It may have been an accident. On the other hand, Apaches may have killed him. Another possibility is that Waltz killed his partner so he wouldn't have to share the treasure. Nothing was ever proved, and the cause of Weiser's death is unknown.

Waltz, who was **referred** to as the Dutchman, kept secret the location of the mine and the hiding place for the gold. He moved to the Phoenix area. There, he became friends with a woman named Julia Thomas. Waltz promised to take her to the Superstition Mountains to show her the secret gold. They planned to go during the spring of 1892. However, Waltz never made it back to the mine.

Will anyone ever locate the gold mine in the Superstition Mountains?

Waltz's house was close to the Salt River, which normally ran dry in the early spring. Strangely, that year rain caused the river to flood. Before he could take Julia to see the gold, Waltz got sick. The rain and dampness from the flooding river caused Waltz to get ill. He died before he and Julia could make the trip.

The Mystery Lives On

Jacob Waltz gave clues to his friend Julia Thomas, but the clues never led to a mine. Did Waltz lie? Did Julia make a mistake? People have studied Waltz's maps and notes. Nobody has been able to find the mine or the hidden gold. For many years, treasure hunters have searched the Superstition Mountains. Nothing has ever been found.

All that is really known about the lost mine is that it is hidden somewhere in the dusty region of the Superstition Mountains. The Superstition Mountains are now part of what is called Lost Dutchman State Park. Visitors can camp, hike, and ride horses through the mountains. Imagine being a lucky vacationer who stumbles across the hiding place. Picture yourself brushing away some bushes and finding shiny gold!

Chapter 6

The World's Treasures

Certain treasures may be of value to an entire nation. For example, in some countries, monuments are created in honor of soldiers who died in wars. This kind of honor gives a country's citizens the opportunity to show appreciation for the achievements of its military heroes.

The country of Japan has its own national treasures that are appreciated by millions of people. In Japan, the title Living National Treasure is the highest honor that can be achieved in the arts. What are these treasures? What makes them so valuable?

The Living National Treasures are actually people! For many centuries, the people of Japan have appreciated fine crafts as well as the people who create these works of art. Pottery, puppet making, fabric design, and music are among the arts that are an important part of Japanese culture. In 1955, the Japanese government started the custom of honoring its Living National Treasures, that is, the impressive craftspeople and performing artists who practice the traditional arts of Japan.

At any one time, approximately 70 individuals are considered to be Japan's treasures. The artists are varied— from weavers to papermakers to actors and so on. These craftspeople and artists receive a small amount of money from the Japanese government. The money helps them continue to work and to teach other people how to create the kinds of work they do. By passing down their knowledge and skills, these individuals play an important role in preserving the culture of the nation. The living treasures have the honor of keeping alive the creative traditions of Japan.

The idea of keeping treasured traditions alive is important in many cultures besides Japan. Imagine a piece of art that has lasted *thousands* of years. Picture a statue that has stood in one place through all that time. It has a history. Many kings, queens, and leaders have come and gone while the statue has been there. It has stood through **military** conflicts as well as terrible disasters. It has been passed down from family to family. It is the only thing left from what was once a great civilization.

A Peek Into Long-Ago Worlds

The country that is now known as Iraq is full of art that has been valued for many years. Many of the treasures there are so old that they are believed to be among the very first pieces of art ever made by humans. This is the place where civilization began. The wheel was invented in what is now Iraq. The first farms were there.

The first written words were recorded in the area. Instead of using letters, people wrote with shapes called cuneiforms. Rather than writing on paper, the people wrote on slabs of clay. These pieces of clay are records of the first time anyone anywhere wrote down what he or she saw and knew. That happened more than 5,000 years ago, which makes the clay records in Iraq very important and very rare. Some of these valuable things can be found in museums. Baghdad is the capital of Iraq. The Baghdad Museum is the home of some of these treasures.

Treasures in the Baghdad Museum are important because they are all that is left from the first cities of the world. These riches reveal how people from the past made sense of the world around them. Today, historians can learn what mattered to people who lived thousands of years ago. The treasures are clues to understanding what life was like at that time.

Stolen Art!

The first Gulf War took place after Iraq invaded the small country of Kuwait. Thirty-two countries joined together to fight against Iraq. During the first Gulf War, which took place in 1991, Iraq's Baghdad Museum was a target for thieves. Important art pieces were stolen from the museum. Then, the thieves sold the stolen art. Their **profits** earned them a lot of money. Iraqi police worked hard to catch the thieves and to **recover** the art pieces. When the art was found, it was returned to the museum where it belonged. The thieves went to jail. Stealing art is a serious crime.

After the second war between Iraq and the United States began in 2003, the museum was **plundered** again. This time, the robbery was worse than before. The museum's most important pieces of art were stolen. Some art was broken or even destroyed. Just one piece missing from the museum would be a terrible loss. However, thousands of pieces of art were stolen from the Baghdad Museum. Losing such an enormous **quantity** of art is heartbreaking.

Crime scene! Ancient objects were destroyed and looted here, at the Baghdad Museum.

Found Treasure

Fortunately, some of the stolen treasures from the museum have been found and returned. One of the most prized sculptures that had been missing was the 3-foot-tall Warka Vase, which was probably made in the Sumerian city of Uruk. Nobody knows who took the vase. It was returned in the trunk of a car!

The Warka Vase was made about 3000 BCE. The decorations on the vase show men giving presents to the goddess Innin. This type of decoration may not seem so rare now, but it's exactly why the vase was worth so much. The carvings on the vase show water, grain, sheep, as well as people. They reveal clues about life 5,000 years ago. The vase is the earliest peek into the daily lives of people who lived so long ago. Sadly, the treasure was brought back to the museum broken. Curators, museum workers who study art, worked at **preserving** the vase and putting it back together.

Other art has been found, too. A marble sculpture called the Lady of Warka is back at the museum. It is one of the museum's most famous pieces. It was made around 3000 BCE, about the same time as the vase. Some art historians think that the sculpture may be Inana, the Sumerian goddess of love and war. This female statue stares as if she knows everyone's secret thoughts. Her eyes used to sparkle with gold and jewels that had been **inserted** into the sculpture. Her eyes are empty spaces now. They were stolen many years ago. However, it is easy to imagine how beautiful she once was. No one had ever dared take the entire sculpture until the second Gulf War. After careful detective work, the Iraqi police found it. They brought it back safely to the museum.

Missing Treasure

Despite some good news about the lost treasure from the Baghdad Museum, there are still many thousands of priceless pieces missing. Among the missing objects is a bronze head of an ancient ruler. This sculpture dates back to 2250 BCE. It is important to artists and historians because it has an unusual mix of styles. The sculpture's face looks very real. However, the ruler's beard doesn't look real at all. His beard looks more like ropes than hair. This combination of styles makes the sculpture special.

The Baghdad Museum is known for its collection of cylinder seals. These are small tubes that have designs around the sides. By **revolving** the tube on soft clay, it leaves the mark of its design behind. These seals were used to mark legal documents. They were used around 1000 BCE. Because the seals are small, they are easy to steal. Then, people can sell the seals and make an easy **profit**.

People have stolen art made from gold in order to melt down the gold. Then, the gold can be sold without anyone ever knowing that it was once a treasure. This is what happened to a beautiful old musical instrument called a lyre. The museum had a lyre with a gold bull on it. The lyre was stolen so the gold could be scraped off it. This beautiful old instrument will never be the same. Searching for the museum's stolen treasure is a huge job. Iraqi police are looking for these objects. The U.S. government is helping them. People who work in museums all over the world are helping in the search. Art experts in universities work to track down stolen treasure. The University of Chicago created a Web site that shows pictures of almost 1,000 pieces that were taken from the Baghdad Museum. The Web site is like a giant poster so that anyone who goes to the site can see what's still missing.

Treasure Belongs to Everyone

Treasure comes in many sizes and forms. You've seen how something as small and simple as a coin can have tremendous worth. Treasure can be as huge and mysterious as a lost city of gold and as important as a **historic** vase. Treasure can also be a key to **informing** people about the past.

A good treasure seeker must do some thinking and planning. A treasure hunter must know the difference between real clues and made-up stories. He or she must find out about the people who hid or stole a treasure. Understanding the past is the key. After all, learning about history helps people understand the present.

Anyone can be a treasure hunter—even you! First, you need a belief that there is a treasure to be found. Ask questions and listen very carefully to the answers. Don't give up the search. When you find your treasure, share it with the world.

Imagine this beautiful bull's head melted into a puddle of gold!

Mysteries of History

by Katherine Scraper

CHAPTER 1

Uncovering History's Secrets

Do you enjoy a mystery? Many people do. Most people are curious when events happen that they cannot explain. What do mystery solvers do? First, they think about everything they already know about a situation. Then, they find out more. Finally, they fit together the information.

History has its share of mysteries. In this book, you will go back in time. You will explore stories of people who lived long ago. You will visit **impressive** places that hold mysterious secrets. For example, think about a group of people living together. A famous writer described their community. He gave a clear **image** of what the people were like and what their country looked like. However, the people mysteriously vanished. What might have happened?

Sometimes mystery solvers have clues to go on. Perhaps something was left behind that can provide information. In fact, some historians and scientists devote years of their lives to studying these puzzles. They study structures, make notes, draw sketches, measure, and do experiments. How do researchers **reconstruct** what happened to groups of people that have disappeared? They trace old legends and travel to places all over the world.

Curious people **continually** seek answers to untold secrets. This book investigates five famous secrets. They range from a mysterious **incident** in American history to a place where entire planes and ships have disappeared.

First, you will visit England. Here, you will examine a cluster of huge rocks called Stonehenge. No written history exists to explain how the stones were moved to that exact spot. Why were they laid out in such careful designs? Who put them there? Next, you will go to Easter Island in the South Pacific. Here, hundreds of unusual statues seem to keep watch over the island. Local legend says the **massive** carved stone figures walked to the island by themselves! Scientists **debate** other ideas about what the statues represent and who placed them on the island.

Returning to the United States, you will visit the site of the Roanoke Colony in present-day North Carolina. Here, more than 100 settlers disappeared without a trace. In fact, their bodies were never found. Where did the men, women, and children go? Did they have any **descendants**? Just off the coast of Florida, you will gaze into the waters of the Bermuda Triangle. In this spot, airplanes have fallen from the sky. Ships and boats have sunk into the dark waters, never to be seen again. Is nature playing a cruel trick with peoples' lives? Why are sailors and pilots still drawn to this area in spite of the reported danger?

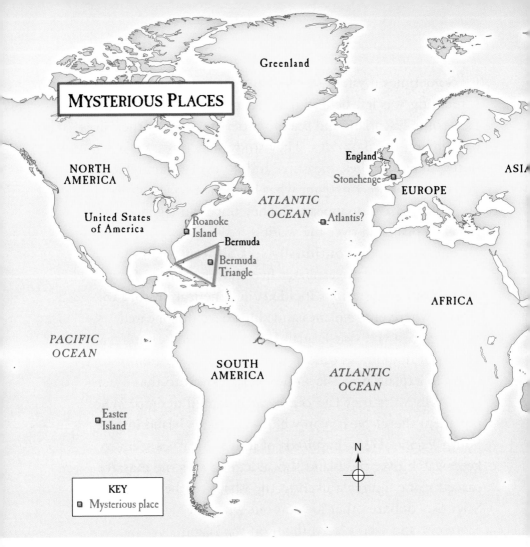

Greenland

MYSTERIOUS PLACES

NORTH
AMERICA

ASIA

England
Stonehenge
EUROPE

United States
of America

ATLANTIC
OCEAN

Roanoke
Island

Atlantis?

Bermuda

Bermuda
Triangle

AFRICA

PACIFIC
OCEAN

SOUTH
AMERICA

ATLANTIC
OCEAN

Easter
Island

N

KEY
▪ Mysterious place

The world is filled with mysterious places to be explored.

Finally, you will attempt to visit the legendary continent of Atlantis. Some people say the sea swallowed up an entire civilization there. Did Atlantis really exist? If not, how could it have been described so precisely? Who is still looking for Atlantis today? Is there a chance it will ever be found? This book will look at possible answers to these and other questions. Think of it as a tour of some of the mysteries of history.

CHAPTER 2

Secrets of Stonehenge

Imagine that you are driving through the grassy hills and plains of south, central England. The sun is shining. Clouds are floating across the sky. Suddenly you see something jutting from the land. You are looking at a ring of stones. The largest pillars are more than 13 feet tall. Shorter stones resting across their tops form archways. This **impressive** sight is known as Stonehenge.

There are more than 900 stone monuments in the United Kingdom. This one is different. The circular shape of its rings of stones makes it special. People from all over the world are drawn to it. As you watch, visitors walk around and through the structure. It seems that someone has gone to a great deal of trouble to collect, shape, and arrange the stones. Some rocks stand alone. Others are in circles or in horseshoe patterns. The rocks are different sizes, shapes, and colors. Streaks of sunlight and shadows appear between them. Also, empty places reveal where stones might have stood long ago.

Archaeologists generally agree that the Stonehenge monument was built and remodeled in three phases. The process took hundreds of years. Think about other buildings you have seen. Picture the modern homes, schools, stores, and offices in your community. Think about the people who built them—people with special training and access to money, transportation, computers, tools, and modern equipment of all kinds. In contrast, Stonehenge has existed for thousands of years. It is prehistoric. Consider how it came into existence. Who might have built Stonehenge? How did the builders choose their location for the circle of stones?

Constructing Stonehenge

The story of Stonehenge began in about 3000 BCE. Fifty-six small holes were dug into the earth, forming a circle. A ditch was dug around the circle of holes. More soil was moved to form a path leading away from the northeast part of the ditch. **Fragments** of deer antlers and oxen shoulder blades have been found at the site. Perhaps these bones were used as digging tools. Next, came 80 blocks of a kind of rock called bluestone. The blocks are arranged in two circles, one inside the other, near the center of the larger circle created by the ditch.

When you first approach Stonehenge, you see towering rocks. They are a type of sandstone called sarsen. First, 30 pillars were erected. Crosspieces, called lintels, then topped the pillars. Five additional pairs of pillars were placed in a horseshoe shape. Lintels are on top of each pair in order to form archways. The pairs of pillars face the circle's northeast entrance.

A block of greenish sandstone was placed at the base of the central archway. Four smaller stones were placed nearby. These four stones form a rectangle. Near the entrance to the archways are two other large stones. Another mysterious feature was added: Someone carved a picture of a dagger on one of the inner sarsen stones.

Visitors to Stonehenge may wonder about many things. For example, carrying the 4-ton bluestones would not have been easy. The stones may have come from Wales, a country more than 100 miles away. Maybe they were floated on rafts from sea to river and were then dragged overland. Perhaps glaciers had already moved the bluestones near the circle. Sarsen stone has been found almost 20 miles away from Stonehenge. Somehow, these 40-ton pillars were moved to the site. Ropes and levers may have been used. Perhaps the sarsens were moved on sleds over winter snow.

Building the structures was hard. First, the stones had to be cut and carved into pillars. Then, they had to be placed upright. Finally, they had to be topped by the lintels. Did you play with blocks when you were younger? Imagine trying to build with a block that is heavier than an elephant.

The identity of the Stonehenge workers is unknown. When the Romans invaded Britain in the first century CE, they met ancient priests called Druids. Early historians believed that either the Druids or the Romans had built the structure. However, their theory was proven wrong. Archaeologists in the twentieth century proved that Stonehenge was **constructed** hundreds of years before the Druids and Romans arrived in the area.

For thousands of years, people have wondered about the mysterious structures of Stonehenge.

Some experts think that each new phase of **construction** was completed by a different group of people that moved to the Stonehenge location. Some people claim that aliens visited Earth long before recorded history. According to this theory, the structure could have been a way to mark the place where aliens landed on Earth. There is no evidence for this theory, though.

The purpose of Stonehenge is yet another mystery. Scholars **analyze** why the inhabitants put so much time and work into creating Stonehenge. What did it mean to them? Were they ever **tempted** to give up? Did each set of builders have the same goal in mind?

Researchers have different ideas about the purpose of Stonehenge. It may have been a temple for religious ceremonies. It may have been a burial site. A more recent theory says that it was used as a calendar to predict movements of the sun, moon, and stars. Parts of Stonehenge line up with the location of sunrise at the summer solstice, the longest day of the year. The holes that were dug may also mark time or seasons in some way. However, other people think that this **concept** is too advanced for humans who lived 5,000 years ago. They wonder if the inhabitants of Stonehenge understood how to measure and calculate such things.

How has Stonehenge changed over time? Nature has had an effect on this place. Climate changes and storms have come and gone. Many of the stones have been worn down or toppled. Also, humans have been at fault, removing many of the stones to use for other purposes. Fortunately, the British government has helped restore and preserve Stonehenge. Thousands of people journey there each year. Visitors wander among the mysterious structures and wonder about the secrets they hold.

CHAPTER 3

Silent Giants of Easter Island

Meet Jakob Roggeveen. He was a Dutch navigator in 1722. In his travels, Roggeveen came upon an island in the South Pacific known as Rapa Nui. The island is more than 2,000 miles away from the nearest mainland. Because Roggeveen arrived on Easter Day, he decided to rename the island Easter Island. The island is shaped like a triangle. Its area is about 64 square miles. An extinct volcano is at each corner of the triangle. There is hardly a tree in sight. Sheep graze on the grasslands. The most unusual thing about Easter Island to Jacob Roggeveen was the presence of its strange stone statues.

What secrets are held by the giant statues that stand guard on Easter Island?

These stone structures are known as Moai. Like silent giants, they are scattered about the countryside. Both the island and the Moai were formed from soft volcanic rock. The type of rock in the statues comes from one of the island's craters, or deep holes.

Long ago, the makers of the statues must have looked at a section of crater rock and thought a lot about how the statues should look. In other words, they **conceptualized** a design. First, the carvers would have considered a rock's shape, cracks, and colors. The next steps would have been cutting and carving the soft rock.

More than 1,000 of the statues on Easter Island were carved in a nearly **identical** style. The giant statues have huge heads and long ears and noses. Some statues once had stone eyes, and some still have inscriptions.

There are still 887 of the original Moai remaining on the island. The smallest statue is little more than 3 feet tall. The largest is more than 70 feet tall. Most of the Moai were placed on platforms **constructed** of stone blocks. Each platform holds between 4 and 15 statues. The platforms were made without the cement mixture that modern bricklayers use to attach bricks. This feat still amazes engineers of today.

One **atypical** Moai is known as the kneeling statue. The carving on it is more realistic than on the other statues. The kneeling statue was found apart from other carved Moai.

Another **atypical** example of Moai is a group of them on a platform on the western shore of the island. The largest statue of the group is in the center of the platform. Two smaller ones stand to the left, an even smaller one to the right, and the smallest to the far right. Each statue is of a different scale and shape. Could this group represent a family? Some people think so.

From Paradise to Wasteland

Easter Island did not always look the way it does today. Like other lands, it has gone through changes. The first inhabitants probably arrived about 400 BCE. There is evidence that the island was filled with giant palm trees at that time. It must have been **tempting** to think the trees would last forever. The wood was used for boats, houses, and fires. Crops were planted. The island population grew to more than 8,000 people. However, several **incidents** changed life on Easter Island.

First of all, with so many people on such a small island, food became scarce. Next, because the palm trees were not replaced as they were used, they became rare. Without trees' roots as an anchor, the soil began to erode. It was harder to grow crops. There was no wood left to build escape boats or even rafts for fishing. The islanders had to fight for the things they needed to live. They began battling one another.

How do the Moai fit into this picture? The creation of the Moai may have been an important part of the problem. The islanders seemed determined to build the statues. Perhaps this goal kept them from caring for their land. Maybe the palm trees were used up even more quickly to make tools for moving the statues. However, the Moai were also affected by the changes on the island. The eroding soil toppled and buried statues. The fighting islanders even destroyed one another's Moai. The **construction** of Moai may have helped to cause the problem. Yet the statues were also victims of the island's difficulties.

In addition, outside **influences** crept in. Smallpox and other diseases from Europe were introduced to the island by travelers. Also, Spanish slave traders invaded and captured men, women, and children. By 1887, only about 100 people were left on the island.

Walking Home

So many questions arise about how the heavy statues were carried about on Easter Island. Somehow they arrived miles away from the crater where they were carved. Perhaps they were rolled on logs coated with a slippery substance. Maybe the statues were placed on the ground face-up and pulled with ropes made out of leaves. It's also possible that they were moved in an upright position. However, if the statues were rocked back and forth to "walk" them to their new homes, those movements may have caused the statues to **fragment**. Island legends claim that the statues walked from the crater to their final resting places. Which theory makes sense to you?

No matter how the statues arrived, getting them to their final location must have been a difficult task. Broken Moai can be seen lying abandoned along the paths of ancient roadways. Many other Moai were never even taken from the crater area. Archaeologists and scientists have tested different methods of moving the statues. Some of the researchers were **inclined** to use only the tools they believe might have been available to the islanders. These tools were probably made of wood, crafted from palm trees.

Mysterious Moai

Debates also go on about why the statues were created. Why did the islanders **continue** to use so much of their time, energy, and resources to carve and move the statues? Who designed the first statue? Perhaps the Moai represent certain people who lived on the island. Many experts think that each statue stands for the head of a family. If so, perhaps each statue was placed in a particular spot to display a family's claim to a section of land.

One big mystery is who made the Moai? Perhaps the current islanders are **descendants** of the artists. On the other hand, other people could have settled on the island. For example, sailors may have landed there and decided to make the island their home. Some people think the statues were placed on the island by an advanced race of people who later vanished. This idea is similar to one of the explanations given about how Stonehenge was built. Again, however, there is no proof for this idea.

There was one way we could have learned something about who made the statues. Remains of carved tablets have been found in caves on the island. The tablets are covered with finely carved figures. These **images** are a form of early picture writing called hieroglyphs. It is reported that missionaries once discovered islanders in the caves. The islanders were hiding from slave traders. The missionaries destroyed most of the tablets. They thought the hieroglyphs were about the inhabitants' religion. The missionaries wanted the islanders to change their beliefs. The destruction likely ruined any written records that might have solved the secret of the Moai.

When archaeologists uncover ancient ruins they might make surprising discoveries about people who lived long ago.

Researching the Moai

Some people make the study of Easter Island their career. For instance, Jo Anne Van Tilburg, of the University of California, Los Angeles (UCLA), has measured and **analyzed** each Moai. She made computer **images** showing how the statues might have been moved.

Van Tilburg has watched the way islanders haul their large canoes by rolling them on logs. She believes the Moai might have been transported that way, too. She built a statue that matched the size of the average Moai. A television show filmed her as she tested her theory. Her plan worked. In a report, Van Tilburg wrote that it would take 40 people to move a **typical** statue and 20 people to erect it. The task would take about 10 days.

Another expert is Patricia Vargas. She works at the University of Chile. Vargas was concerned about some of the Moai. Fifteen statues had been knocked down and damaged by a huge storm. She gathered a crew of 40 people to erect the Moai again. The group used the most advanced crane available. The project took four years.

The work of each of these women has had a distinct **influence** on the study of the island. Each woman had different ways of studying the island and its statues. However, both women have similar feelings about what they learned. They admire the clever, skillful early movers. They are **impressed** by the islanders' determination to succeed in carving and moving these statues.

Research **continues**. The mystery **tempts** people to keep trying to find answers. That is not so easy. Sometimes figuring out the answer to one question leads to even more questions. In fact, Patricia Vargas has said that the more she works on Easter Island, the less she feels she knows.

CHAPTER 4

Lost Colony of Roanoke

Like the Easter Island puzzle, the story of Roanoke is filled with mysteries. Roanoke Colony was settled more than 400 years ago on an island that is near present-day North Carolina. Most of the knowledge of Roanoke that exists comes from copies of journals, letters, and maps, as well as drawings from early travelers.

The story begins in England during the reign of Queen Elizabeth I, who ruled from 1558 to 1603. Sir Walter Raleigh, full of energy and ideas, wanted to serve the queen. In 1584, he sent explorers out to find a new land to settle. Two of them returned with news of a small island. They described the friendly Croatoan people who lived there. The explorers told of rich soil, delicious grapes, sweet-smelling woods, and abundant fish and wild animals. The queen was **impressed**. She told Raleigh to move ahead with his plans.

Sir Walter Raleigh was a favorite of Queen Elizabeth. The next King of England, James I, ordered Raleigh to be beheaded.

Walter Raleigh selected a group of 100 men, mostly soldiers. One was John White, an artist and mapmaker. The men planned to set up a colony. They were under the direction of Sir Richard Grenville and Ralph Lane. They sailed from England in seven ships. In late summer of 1585, they landed on Roanoke Island. Grenville left soon after to return to England for supplies. Lane stayed with the others to **construct** houses and a fort.

While on the island, the new settlers made some mistakes. The most serious error was to anger the Native Americans on whom they relied for help, food, and supplies. In one **incident**, a Native American village was burned over a stolen cup. The situation was serious.

A ship from England stopped by the colony in 1586. The colonists decided to board the ship and return home. If they had stayed in Roanoke for just a few days longer, they would have been able to welcome Grenville. He finally arrived with much-needed supplies. Grenville was surprised the settlement was empty. When he left Roanoke the next time Grenville left 15 men there to protect the settlement. The new settlers had enough supplies to last two years.

In 1587, Walter Raleigh sent another group of settlers to Roanoke. This time he included men, women, and children. He **tempted** the travelers by promising each family 500 acres in the new land. John White would be the governor. White took along his daughter Eleanor and her husband Ananias Dare. The Dares were expecting a baby.

The leaders knew about the experiences of the first colony. They were concerned about the conditions in Roanoke. They decided to settle farther north in what is now the Chesapeake Bay area. However, the pilot of the fleet, who had also piloted the first trip, insisted that his instructions were to return to Roanoke.

Return to Roanoke

Governor White and his aides had planned to visit Roanoke anyway. They wanted to talk to the 15 men left by Grenville to see how they had fared. White and his men were eager to find out what the Roanoke settlers had learned. When they reached the settlement, they were in for a huge surprise: No one was there.

The houses were still standing, but they were all empty. The fort was in **fragments**. Upon further search, the new settlers found the bones of one of the men. There was no sign of the other men. Questions and fear must have filled their minds. They did not know that the other 14 men would never be seen or heard from again. Even worse, a nearly **identical** situation was about to occur among their own people.

Putting his concerns aside, Governor White focused on the tasks at hand. Many of the new colonists could settle into the existing houses, but other homes needed to be **constructed**. Food and supplies were scarce.

Roanoke colonists used tools such as these to build houses and forts.

Then, there was more trouble. One of the governor's assistants was killed by a group of Native Americans. The settlers decided to seek revenge, but the group responsible had already fled. In their place were friendly Croatoans hunting for food. The settlers accidentally attacked the wrong people. Only with the help of a friendly chief were the new colonists able to make peace once again with their neighbors.

In the midst of all the problems, an event of great joy occurred. On August 18, 1587, Eleanor Dare gave birth to a daughter. She was named Virginia and was the first child born of English parents in America. The birth of Governor White's granddaughter became the hopeful symbol of a new nation that would rise in North America.

As time passed, it became clear that the colony needed more food and materials. Someone had to return to England for supplies. As governor of the colony, White's **inclination** was to stay with his people. However, he was the one chosen to make the trip.

At that time, the colonists had once again begun discussing moving to the north. Before the governor sailed, he and the colonists worked out a secret code. If the colonists did leave Roanoke Island, they were to carve on a tree the name of their new location. If the move resulted from an attack, they were to carve a cross over the letters. Governor White left his daughter, son-in-law, newborn granddaughter, and more than 100 other colonists. He promised to be back soon.

Typically, the trip to England and back would have taken a few months. However, stormy seas slowed the passage. After his arrival in England, a war with Spain delayed the governor's return trip for three more years. White did not return to Roanoke until 1590. By then, it was too late.

Gone!

Imagine Governor John White's return to Roanoke Island. Picture him as he stepped onto the beach and **continued** along the path. He was back at the colony he had been forced to leave three years earlier. In fact, the day he returned was his granddaughter Virginia's third birthday.

When White reached the settlement, he found no sign of human life. The people were gone. Their houses were gone as well. All that he found was tall grass and the tree-trunk walls of a new fort. He must have been relieved to see that there were no signs of attack. However, where was everyone?

White remembered the code. He searched the trees for a clue to where the colonists had gone. On one of the fort trees, he found the carved letters CRO. Nearby there was another inscription: the word CROATOAN.

After more than 400 years, the fate of the Roanoke colonists is still a puzzle.

White must have been relieved to see there was not a cross on either sign. He thought the marks on the trees meant the settlers had moved to the neighboring Croatoan Island. The island was about 50 miles to the south. This surprised him. The colonists had only discussed moving north.

White made plans to visit Croatoan Island, but he had problems once again. A sudden severe storm forced the ships to put out to sea and return to England. White was never able to return to the Roanoke Island again. He never learned what happened to his family and the colony.

Theories

From England, Sir Walter Raleigh organized trips to search for the lost colonists. The last trip was made in 1602. In 1607, a group of English men, women, and children arrived. They built a new settlement called Jamestown, in what is now Virginia. The Jamestown settlers also tried to locate the earlier settlers. Not a survivor was ever found. Many people have tried to **conceptualize** what may have happened, based on their own theories.

Scientists believe that the colonists faced one of the worst dry spells in the area's history. Without rain, food would have become very scarce. There was already a history of trouble with the Native Americans. Maybe the colonists were killed over food. If so, how were the signs of battle hidden? Perhaps clues lay beneath the grass.

Many people believe the settlers joined neighboring Native American groups or were captured by them. If the settlers did live among the Native Americans, it would help explain changes in the native people's appearance, names, languages, and tools through the years. Some of the tribal **descendants** agree with this idea. Others wonder whether so few people could have had such an **influence**.

Some people say that the colonists did move to Croatoan Island then split into two groups. One group may have stayed and gradually joined the native people there. The other group may have moved north. One theory is that the Native American chief, Powhatan, killed the northern group. He may have been afraid that the Roanoke survivors would combine with the new Jamestown colonists and overpower him. Other historians question these ideas and say they are **debatable**. They say that if the colonists had moved on their own, they would have contacted Governor White.

When Governor White left the colony to go to England for supplies, he had left a small boat for the colonists to use. Perhaps they tried to return to England in it. Maybe they were lost at sea. On the other hand, the settlers may have known that this idea was too foolish. Many questions remain about the fate of the Roanoke colonists.

Between 1937 and 1940, stone tablets were found in the area. The tablets had inscriptions that described the colonists' travels. Also, some of the writing told of the death of Eleanor Dare. Did the Roanoke settlers leave a history after all? However, upon **analysis**, the tablets appeared to be fakes. Most people are **inclined** to believe the tablets were a joke. Nobody is sure who made them. The tablets just add to the mysteries of Roanoke.

Fort Raleigh is now a National Historic Site in North Carolina. Visitors view historical items found in the area. Curious people think about and try to solve the mysteries of the lost colony of Roanoke.

What was held in these colorful pots found by archaeologists searching for clues about the lost colony?

CHAPTER 5

Strange Zone of the Bermuda Triangle

On a globe, put your finger at the tip of Florida. Trace a line across to Bermuda. Then, go to Puerto Rico and back to Florida. Some people refuse to travel inside this imaginary triangle, which is known as the Bermuda Triangle. Why? Over the years, airplanes and ships have sunk into the ocean in this area for unknown reasons. Few of them call for help. Most have never been found.

Flight 19

On December 5, 1945, five navy airplanes called Avengers left Fort Lauderdale, Florida. Their mission was named Flight 19. The planes were to fly east, then north, then southwest to return home. Around 4:00 p.m., a radio message came through. The commander of the mission said his compasses had stopped working. Also, he could not see any familiar landmarks. The commander was not sure where he was. Contact was spotty after that. The ground crew was concerned. If Flight 19 was lost, the planes might run out of fuel and be forced to **descend**. The pilots would have to exit the planes in parachutes.

At that time, air stations did not have reliable equipment to track **images** of planes. Rescue airplanes searched for the Avengers. Air station workers were alarmed when they could not radio one of the airplanes, a Martin Mariner. Sailors at sea reported an explosion and a pool of oil. Air station workers feared it was caused by the Mariner. However, the search for the lost Avengers **continued**, using hundreds of airplanes and ships. Neither the Mariner nor the other Avengers—or their passengers—were ever found.

Other Unexplained Events

What caused so many things to go wrong that day? Some people might say, "Accidents happen." At first, the navy blamed the **incident** on pilot mistakes. Later, that changed. The navy stated that Flight 19 was lost for "causes or reasons unknown." It also believed that the Mariner exploded soon after takeoff.

However, there have been other **incidents** involving airplanes and ships that were lost in the Bermuda Triangle. Some events happened even before the Avenger disaster. For example, a ship called the USS *Cyclops* vanished in 1918. Other **incidents** took place later. A ship called the *Marine Sulphur Queen* disappeared in 1963. Various records have been kept during the past century. Some reports show dozens of ships and aircraft lost. Others show hundreds.

The area got its nickname from an article that appeared in a magazine called *Argosy* in 1964. The article was called "The Deadly Bermuda Triangle." Since then, countless experts have discussed the topic. The Bermuda Triangle has been the subject of books, television shows, Web sites, and even a movie. Some people explore the triangle as their life's work.

Why did the commander of Flight 19 think he was flying toward Fort Lauderdale when he was actually heading out to sea?

Just a Legend?

Many experts think that the idea of disasters taking place within the Bermuda Triangle is just a legend. After all, accidents can happen anywhere and for many reasons. For example, bad weather can cause problems. Mechanical difficulties can occur, such as when the Avengers' compasses did not work. Humans make mistakes, too, which can lead to fatal results.

For many, it is **tempting** to blame UFOs. In the movie *Close Encounters of the Third Kind,* the Avengers return to Earth from a spaceship. Some people believe the area is a secret passage that leads to another place and time! Many theories exist to try to explain the mysteries of the Bermuda Triangle.

A **massive** warm ocean current called the Gulf Stream flows through the Bermuda Triangle. The current is fast-moving and rough. Perhaps it causes some accidents. Waterspouts are also common. A waterspout is a swirling column of water like a tornado on water. Waterspouts can pull water high into the sky.

Many scientists are **inclining** toward a newer theory. When **analyzing** the ocean bed, they found methane gas on the ocean floor. If the gas bubbles up to the surface of the ocean it could affect both the water and the sky above it. Maybe the gas causes engines in ships and planes to explode.

The U.S. government states that it does not recognize the Bermuda Triangle as an official name. The government does not keep an official file on the area. It is the experience of the Coast Guard that human error can cause disasters. Nature can also cause disasters at sea. Coast Guard crews answer distress calls every day. To the Coast Guard, it is no surprise many problems occur in such a heavily traveled area.

CHAPTER 6

Atlantis: Fact or Fiction?

Of all the mysterious places described in this book, the one that is the most **debated** is Atlantis. Atlantis has been called a fable, a myth, and a legend. It has also been called "a great and wonderful empire." People the world over study about it, and search for it. An equal number of people say it does not exist, and it never did. What exactly is Atlantis?

In the third century BCE, the Greek writer Plato wrote about a continent of strong and charming men, women, and children. The people were intelligent and kind. They were well governed. Women had equal rights with men. The people of Atlantis used technology to become powerful leaders in the world. Plato said that the continent had existed some 10,000 years earlier. He said it was located to the west of the Straits of Gibraltar, where the Mediterranean Sea meets the Atlantic Ocean. Minerals, plants, and animals filled the land. Hot and cold springs flowed from the ground. The capital city was built with circular walls and canals. The climate was so favorable that crops could be harvested twice each year. Water from rivers and streams was collected in one of the canals for watering summer crops. Winter rainfalls meant that winter crops received enough water. In the middle of the city was a great temple on a hill.

Life on Atlantis changed, however. According to Plato, after many years of wealth and happiness, the people became greedy and lazy. Some writers have said the people of Atlantis were being punished for their attitude by what happened next. Tragedy struck Atlantis. A violent earthquake shook the area and caused huge tidal waves. The disasters destroyed the continent in one day and one night, plunging it into the ocean. Atlantis had vanished forever.

Search for Atlantis

Plato's sad tale of Atlantis has **tempted** explorers everywhere. Based on the location that Plato described, many look to the Azores Islands, off the coast of Portugal. In fact, some people think that the islands are the actual mountain peaks of Atlantis.

Archaeologists say that the lower layers of the Azores were above water at one time. When a period in history called the Ice Age drew to a close, sheets of ice in the ocean began to melt. The sea level gradually rose, causing lands to flood. However, Atlantis could not have been destroyed in a single day and night in this way. Also, the ocean floor under the Azores shows no signs of a sunken continent. The size of the Azores does not fit Plato's story either. Although long ago it is possible that land was measured differently from the way it is today.

Where else could Atlantis have been? Plato said that Atlantis was west of the Straits of Gibraltar. As it has not been discovered to the west, some people have looked to the east instead. Located there is the island of Thera. Over the years, archaeologists have uncovered ancient buildings, tools, and art on Thera. Archaeologists agree that the people who lived on Thera were ahead of their time. Many say that the culture of Thera was **identical** to Plato's description of the culture of Atlantis.

Here are some examples of how Atlantis and Thera were alike: Like Atlantis, Thera suffered a disaster. A nearby volcano erupted in about 1500 BCE. That volcano probably caused **massive** tidal waves and killed thousands of people. However, the timing of the Thera volcano does not agree with Plato's story. Many people blame the mix-up on the storytellers. Perhaps in repeating the story, the wrong date was passed on. Could Thera be the true Atlantis?

A more recent theory came about when the Bimini Wall was discovered in the 1960s. The wall is made of rows of columns. The wall is located under the water within the Bahamas, which are a group of islands near Florida. Some believe the columns are from the buildings of Atlantis. Many scientists disagree. Books have been written about the area. Movies have been filmed there. Visitors flock to the site.

Another theory is that Atlantis was in Antarctica at a warmer time. The continent might have been frozen inside a glacier and pushed under the ocean. If so, it is waiting to be discovered.

Where was Atlantis? So far, no definite answers have been found. There are many opinions, all based on different theories. Some critics say that experts simply change story details to fit their theories.

Could Atlantis still be waiting to be discovered underwater?

Many artists have tried to imagine what Atlantis looked like.

Will We Ever Know?

Plato's story about Atlantis is read and discussed today. It is not very long, yet it has inspired thousands of other authors. Many stories, articles, and books have been written about the **concept** of the lost city. There have also been television specials and movies for both adults and children. As Atlantis was before Plato's time, how did he learn the story? He stated that it came from a friend. His friend heard it from ancestors, who in turn heard it from an Egyptian priest.

As you have read, the idea of Atlantis is **debatable**. It might be fact or fiction. Scientists, archaeologists, and explorers are either believers or disbelievers. Many hope that Atlantis is real, and some hope to be the ones to discover it.

Experts who do not believe in Atlantis may claim that Plato was using **imagery**. In this way of thinking about the story, Plato's tale of Atlantis was meant to teach a lesson. He wanted to show what could happen when people become greedy. These critics say the story is no different from the fairy tales of long ago that were written to teach children the importance of having good manners or being clever. Others **debate** that there would have been no need for Plato to fill in so many vivid details if he was simply using the story as an example. Also, Plato mentioned several times that he was stating true facts. Why would he have said that if it were not so? Would he have said it was a true story if he made it up?

Perhaps the Atlantis story is entirely true. In contrast, it might be totally false. A third possibility is that it was based on fact but contains innocent mistakes. The mystery of Atlantis may never be solved.

Connections

It is appropriate to end this tour of history's mysteries here. Why? The tale of Atlantis has ties to other mysteries. In fact, Atlantis is like a magnet for theories about mysterious places. Atlantis has been linked to *all* of the other stories in this book.

Many people believe that the builders of Stonehenge came from Atlantis. The same conclusion has been made about the statues on Easter Island. Perhaps the people fled the flooding continent in ships and were scattered about the world. They may have settled in new, unknown lands. Because they were advanced in many ways, their design and **construction** skills could have been put to good use. Perhaps the former residents of Atlantis and their **descendants** built the monuments as places of worship.

The stories of Roanoke and Atlantis are centuries apart. However, they often share space in books about lost civilizations. What do the two cultures have in common? Both civilizations disappeared without an explanation. For Roanoke, there were clues to follow. For Atlantis, only a story existed. Which mystery is harder to explain?

Believe it or not, the Bermuda Triangle is considered by many to be the final resting place of the sunken Atlantis. Many say that the same force that pulled the continent underwater is working today to pull down planes and ships. Remember the Bimini Wall? It lies within the Bermuda Triangle. Can you see how that adds to its mystery? The stories that are told about Atlantis are likely to **continue** until someone can prove that they are wrong.

Everyone loves a good mystery. People like to use their imaginations. They enjoy making discoveries. It is interesting to learn and think about new ideas or to form theories. However, people should not be too impressionable. Like critics, people should not believe everything they hear or read. On the other hand, it is good to keep an open mind and be willing to think about subjects that are out of the ordinary. A good balance is to be led by curiosity but to **continue** to depend on facts and research.

Think of the stories of Stonehenge, Easter Island, Roanoke, the Bermuda Triangle, and Atlantis. Are you **tempted** to learn more about these mysterious places? If so, you can find out more by reading books, magazines, and newspapers. Begin watching and listening for new stories as well. As discoveries are made, you will hear of these places again and again. Who knows? Perhaps someday you will be the one to solve a puzzle that has captured the minds and hearts of people throughout the centuries.

Glossary

analyzed something examined carefully to identify its various parts. An **analysis** is a method of studying the important parts of something.

atypical unusual. **Typical** means normal. **Typically** means what usually happens.

concept an idea. To **conceptualize** is to think about an idea and try to picture it.

conquest something gained by force

construction the act of making or building something. **Reconstruct** means to put something back together the way it was originally made or to figure out a past chain of events. To **construct** something is to make or build it.

continue to keep on going. **Continually** means frequently or without stopping.

credit praise for something done or achieved

debate to discuss or argue. A **debate** is also a discussion in which each side has a different argument or solution. Something that is **debatable** can be thought about in many different ways with no obvious right or wrong answer.

defeat to win over an enemy

descendants people who are born to a particular ancestor. To **descend** is to move down.

extend to spread or stretch out. Something that has been **extended** has been made longer in length or time.

fragment to break into small parts. **Fragments** are small pieces.

historic something worthy of being noticed due to its place in a past event

identical just the same as another thing

images things that represent something else, such as statues or pictures. **Imagery** is a picture or a description in your mind.

impressive making you take notice, usually in a positive way. If you are **impressed**, you have been affected by something.

incidents things that happen

inclined tending toward a certain way of thinking or doing something. An **inclination** is the way a person is likely to think or behave.

increase to make something larger in number or amount. If something is **increased** it has been added to or made larger.

Influence the power to produce an effect

inform to give facts, or knowledge, to someone. An **informed** person has been told what he or she needs to know.

insert to put something in something else. An item that is **inserted** has been placed inside another item.

massive huge, covering a large area

military armed forces or a group of soldiers

plundered robbed and spoiled. To **plunder** means to destroy and steal.

preserve to keep something safe and free from damage. If something is **preserved** it has been protected from harm. **Preserving** something is keeping it safe.

profit to gain wealth

quantity an amount or number of something

recover to bring back to normal. A **recovery** is the return to a normal state.

referred named or talked about. To **refer** is to speak of someone or something.

revolve to turn around in a circle. **Revolving** means moving in a circle or orbit.

tempted being convinced to do something, often involving a questionable decision. If something is **tempting**, you are thinking strongly about it. Something that **tempts** you forces your attention on it.

Index